More Parables
for
Little People

by
Larry Castagnola S.J.

Resource Publications, Inc.
160 East Virginia Street, Suite 290
San Jose, California 95112

Editorial Director: Kenneth Guentert
Production Editor: Elizabeth J. Asborno
Cover Design and Production: Ron Niewald
Illustrations: Nancy LaBerge Muren
Production Assistant: Allison Cunningham

Library of Congress Cataloging-in-Publication Data
Castagnola, Lawrence A.
　　More Parables For Little People.

　　Summary: Sixteen stories about animals and people, some of which
are based on Biblical stories but do not use the names of the original
characters, convey basic truths of Christian behavior.
　　Children's stories, American. [1. Christian life — Fiction. 2. Short
stories] I. Muren, Nancy LaBerge, ill. II. Title
PZ7.C26858Mo 1987 [Fic]　　　　　　　　　　　　　　87-62532
ISBN 0-89390-095-8 (pbk.)

5 4 3

Contents

Introduction

"Do you have a children's story with a happy, positive message?" This was a question I often asked of librarians and educators of the young as I tried to prepare my weekly "Children's Mass" in Sacramento, California. Like so many parents, I grew weary of trying to pull out some sound moral themes from traditional stories, which glorify punishment, racism, vengeance, and self-righteousness.

In volume II of Parables For Little People, I continue to answer my own question to the librarians and educators. The first seven stories deal generally with the Jesus themes of caring, sharing, non-violence, and human rights. The remaining stories enter more directly into the New Testament parables, sayings, and historical narratives. While I embellish the biblical narratives with literary fantasy, I try to remain true to the Gospel message.

I hope this new volume of Parables will be of help to parents and teachers searching for alternatives to the main plot of so many children's stories of today: death from a laser beam. And though I wrote these stories for the comprehension of young readers, they are good for the little people of all ages.

Flowerboy

At the age of 9, Sanya spent most of his time in the street. While most children his age were being told by their parents to stay out of the street, Sanya stood in the middle of a busy boulevard selling flowers. When cars stopped at the red light, Sanya would go to each one and say, "Flowers, I have beautiful flowers for a dime." After selling all his flowers, Sanya would return home to his parents with the few dollars he had earned. The money was always spent for rice and vegetables.

Sanya and his parents lived in a one-room hut made of cardboard, tree branches, and a few pieces of sheet metal. Their house had no running water or electricity. It was the way the poor people in his country lived.

Sanya only had patched clothes to wear to school. Even though his clothes were always neat and clean, some of the other children made fun of him. They would say things like, "Sanya lives in a slum; Sanya is a bum." Sanya usually didn't answer the children who made fun of him. But one day when a boy named Obmar called his parents names, Sanya punched him. He gave Obmar a black eye. That evening Sanya told his parents what happened at school. His father said, "Don't worry if others make fun of you because you're poor. You don't have to punch anyone because they call you or us names. They only hurt themselves by their name calling. It's okay to be poor. I want you to respect everyone — especially the poor, the handicapped, and the old people."

After saying this, Sanya's father told him the story of a rich man who hoarded tons of food because he was always afraid of being hungry. The rich man wouldn't even give away stale bread to the poor beggars. The story ended with the rich man dying at an early age from a stroke that the doctors said came from worry.

Sanya was impressed by the story — even though he knew that many beggars died of starvation at an early age.

The next day Sanya was selling his flowers as usual. Across the street from where he was, an old, disabled man with homemade crutches was trying to catch a bus. But every time he tried to climb the bus steps, people would crowd in front of him. And the bus drivers were too impatient to wait the extra minute it took for him to get on the bus. So they closed their doors on him and left him standing alone in the street.

Sanya felt anger toward the bus drivers and the people who wouldn't help the man. He counted the money he earned for the day: two dollars. He called a taxi driver, gave him the two dollars, and asked him to take the disabled man where he wanted to go.

When Sanya got home that evening, he told his parents how he gave all his earnings to help the disabled man. His mother smiled, but his father's face was red with anger.

"That was stupid," shouted his father. "How are we going to eat tonight? Poor people don't use taxis."

Sanya hung his head in shame. He did not know how to answer his father. He thought he had done the right thing.

Sanya's mother now was angry — not at Sanya but at her husband. She said, "Yesterday, you told our son to respect the poor, the disabled, and the old people. You even told him the story of the rich man who died from worry about his money. Today in your anger with Sanya you have become the rich man of your story. We can go one evening without eating. But we cannot go for long without our pride and dignity."

The father's face changed from red to its normal color of brown. Putting his arm around his son he said, "Your mother is right. It is easy for me to give speeches, but hard to practice what I preach."

As he was saying this, someone knocked on the door of their house. It was the father of Obmar, the boy who had made fun of Sanya at school.

"I saw Sanya help the old man today," said the visitor. "I was very impressed. I said to myself, "This boy has something that no money can buy. I only wish my son could be like Sanya."

Saying this the man motioned for his son to come in the house. Obmar gave Sanya a box of groceries and said he was sorry for what he said at school. Sanya too apologized for giving him the black eye.

Sanya accepted the present and shook hands with the boy who was once a brat. He went to bed that evening thinking of all the good things that happened to him as a result of the one little thing he did for a disabled man trying to catch a bus.

LaBerge Muren

The Silkworms Riddle

Elephant called together his best friends: Porcupine, Skunk, and Bat. "I'm bored," he yawned. "So let's have some fun. Let's have a contest. The winner will get a free ride across the forest on my back."

"That sounds like fun," said his three friends. "But are you sure you want to give one of us a ride on your back?"

"My promises are always good," said Elephant. "Now listen to the rules of the contest. As you have noticed, the Hunter doesn't bother us. He no longer comes to our forest. The one who gives me the best answer to 'Why the Hunter doesn't bother us' wins the prize."

"Sounds easy enough," said Porcupine.

"Let the contest begin," bellowed Elephant.

Bat was the first to speak: "The Hunter doesn't bother us anymore because I scared him away. When the Hunter sees me he thinks of Dracula, the human bat who loves blood."

"Not a bad explanation," said Elephant. "You might win the contest."

"I have a better explanation," bragged Porcupine, who spoke next. "Hunter is really afraid of me. Look at my 20,000 needle-like spears. I am a one-man army. I could turn the Hunter into a human pincushion. Dracula, the human bat, is only for the movies. I am real. The Hunter is afraid of me, not Bat."

Elephant liked Porcupine's reason. "Can you beat that reason?" he asked Skunk.

"Do you mind if I sing a song about why the Hunter no longer comes to the forest?" asked Skunk.

The forest creatures looked at each other with puzzlement as Skunk began to sing:

"Oh say can you see
Why Hunter runs from me.
He doesn't want my skin to sell
For he can't stand my smell."

Elephant liked Skunk's song. He thought all the animals gave good reasons why the Hunter no longer came to the forest. As he was trying to decide who won the contest, a silkworm lowered himself from a branch and looked Elephant in the eye.

"May I join your contest?" asked Silkworm.

"Why not?" answered Elephant. "It will be fun to hear the argument of a puny, little worm who couldn't scare a flea."

Like Skunk, Silkworm gave his explanation with a song:

"Mean Hunter doesn't fear
Skunk's smell or Porcu's spear.
He will take what he wants
Be it Bats or Elephants."

The animals were puzzled by the Silkworm's song. The Silkworm continued with a riddle for a hint.

"The thing that chased away the Hunter is none of us. It is a monster made of paper."

"What color is this Monster?" asked Skunk.

"It's green," answered Silkworm.

"How big is it?" asked Bat.

"It's small enough to hide under your wings."

The hints didn't help. Elephant and his friends thought and thought, but they couldn't come up with the answer to Silkworm's riddle. They asked for the answer.

"Before I give you the answer," said Silkworm, "I want to ask you all a question. Why did Hunter kill Bear, Racoon and Kangaroo, Mink and Fox? Do you know?"

"That's easy," answered Elephant. "For their skins and furs."

"You're right," said Silkworm. "You're just lucky he didn't get your tusks."

"Get to the point, Silkworm," commanded Elephant. "What or who is this monster that chased away Hunter?"

"It's 'Monster Money,' alias 'Green Stuff.'"

"We still don't understand," said the animals, who were tired of the Silkworm's riddles.

"There's no riddle, my friends," said the confident Silkworm. "When Hunter discovered me, he saw he could make clothes that were beautiful and cheap. He discovered that I could make more money for him by spinning my silk. So it was the money he made from me and my family that saved your hides."

Elephant liked the Silkworm's explanation and declared him the winner of the contest. Bat, Skunk, and Porcupine began to complain but stopped when Silkworm shouted: "I'm not greedy. I'll share my prize with all of you — that's if Elephant doesn't mind."

"Sounds cool," said Elephant.

As the shadows began to fall along the edge of the forest, the fireflies provided an escort to the strange sight of an elephant giving a ride to a bat, a skunk, a porcupine, and a silkworm.

LaBerge Muren

The
Robot's
magic

There once was a girl whose only friends were plastic dolls. Her name was Barbie (which is short for Barbara).

Barbie's parents wanted her to have real, live friends. So on Valentine's Day, they would invite the other children from the neighborhood to their home for a party. But Barbie would just throw candy at the children and call them bad names. Barbie, it seems, didn't want any friends. She didn't like the idea of sharing candy or anything else. So whenever her parents invited other children to her home, she acted the same way. After the third party, her parents could find no children to come to their home.

Barbie's parents were worried about her bad behavior. In order to help her, they sent her to an expensive place called a "finishing school." This was a school that specialized in teaching children good manners. Barbie was expelled from this school the first day for kicking the principal. The principal said to her parents: "Your child has problems." (The principal wanted to say to her parents: "Your child is a devil"; but in order to be polite, simply said "Your child has problems.")

"We know she has problems," said her parents. "That's why we sent her here."

"I'm dreadfully sorry," said the principal, "but Barbie is too out of control for us to help. Perhaps you can get some advice from a psychiatrist."

So Barbie's parents took her to a psychiatrist. He, too, got a good kick in the shins from Barbie, who treated adults worse than children.

"My advice to you," said the psychiatrist, "is to take your child home and give her an old-fashioned spanking."

Barbie's parents paid the psychiatrist for his time but did not take his advice. They did not believe in spanking.

"Maybe when she starts going to school, she will learn to get along," reasoned her parents. "For now we'll just leave her alone."

It happened one day that Barbie's father went on a business trip to Tokyo, Japan, and met an interesting man named "Father of Robots." This man had also had problems with his daughter at one time. He was able to give Barbie's father some help.

"I can loan you my robot, Criada," said Father of Robots. "I made her to help my daughter, who was exactly like your daughter."

Barbie's father was excited and happy about getting Criada, the helper robot, for Barbie.

"I have just one worry," said Barbie's father to the Father of Robots. "Will Criada ever hurt Barbie? I don't believe in spanking."

"Don't worry," said Father of Robots. "My robots are not programmed to hate or hurt. Trust me."

Criada went with Barbie's father to the U.S.A. For the first few days, she got along well with Barbie. She played dolls with her and helped her with her house chores. But after a few days, things didn't go so well. Barbie began to kick Criada and call her names. When Barbie called her a "metallic moron," Criada walked out of the house. She didn't return that evening.

Barbie's father was fearful for the safety of Criada, who was not used to the U.S.A. He called the local police station to file a "missing persons report."

"Criada, my baby-sitter, ran away," he told the police.

"How old is she?" asked the police.

"About three years old," answered Barbie's father.

"What color hair does she have?" asked the policeman, who didn't understand the first answer but kept on asking questions.

"Her hair is grey, the color of metal."

"I suppose she is a robot," said the policeman.

"Yes," answered Barbie's father.

"Well, I only take the missing person reports for creatures from outer space and leprechauns," answered the angry policeman, as he hung up.

Barbie's father then dialed long distance to the Father of Robots. He told him the story of Criada's runaway.

"Don't worry," said the robotmaker. "This happened once to my daughter. Criada simply went away for a few days to re-program herself. She will self-adjust. But I must warn you, she may now show anger. A red light will flash in her earrings if she is getting angry. Let that be a signal for your child to apologize. When the light in her earrings flashes, Barbie must say the magic words: 'I'm sorry.' But remember, she must *mean* the words."

After a few days, Criada did come back. The first thing she did was have a talk with Barbie. She explained about her earrings that lit up and all about the magic words.

Barbie was alright for a few days, but then went back to her old ways of kicking and calling names. Criada's earrings lit up — a bright red. Barbie saw the lights go on but paid no attention.

Criada picked up Barbie in her metal arms and held her for the first time.

"I'm not going to let you go until you say the magic words and *mean* them!" said Criada.

Barbie screamed and screamed: "Let me down, you pile of scrap metal!" Her parents came into the room to see what was wrong.

"Don't hurt her!" they said to Criada.

"Don't worry!" said the robot. "I'm in control of myself and your darling."

Barbie continued to kick and scream. But Criada kept holding her saying, "I'm waiting for the magic words."

After a half hour of struggling, Barbie finally said, "I'm sorry." But Criada did not let her down. Nor did the lights in her earrings turn off.

"I'm not like humans," warned Criada. "I know when you *mean* your words. The Father of Robots equipped me with lie detector equipment."

The struggle went on for several hours. There were times when Barbie's parents came into the room and said, "Enough! Let her down! She must go to bed!" But Criada did not listen to Barbie's parents. She just kept holding on to Barbie. And that's where Barbie slept for the night — in Criada's arms.

When daylight came the next morning, Barbie looked into Criada's eyes and said, "I'm sorry." This time she really meant the magic words.

Criada brought Barbie to her parents, who were watching T.V.

"Your daughter is cured. It wasn't easy. But if you want her to stay cured, you have to change your behavior too."

Why do you say *we* must change *our* behavior? We don't kick people or call them names."

"I know. But you don't spend any time with your daughter. Maybe you could spend a little time holding her. Try it before she goes back to her old ways."

After saying this Criada disappeared. And, as she was programmed to do, she took a plane back to Tokyo.

Firegirl

One day Al's teacher asked him, "Can a sister be a boy's best friend?" Al had no problem with the answer. He said, "Yes." The other boys in the class laughed, but Al meant his answer. His sister, Ann Marie, was his best friend and he was not ashamed of it. He and his sister played on the same teams, went to the same places, and sang in the same choir. Their parents had encouraged them to do things together.

One thing that Ann Marie was not allowed to do with her brother was serve Mass. This was a special privilege in her church for boys only. There was no such thing as an "altar girl." When Ann Marie asked her pastor, Father Sam, if she could serve Mass, she was told it couldn't be done. He explained to her the meaning of "tradition."

Father Sam felt bad that he could not allow Ann Marie to serve at the altar, but rules were rules. Girls weren't boys.

When Al took his turn serving Mass, Ann Marie would go with him to the church. But she could not serve with him at the altar. She didn't feel jealous of her brother. She just felt left out. She played on all his teams and sang in the same choir. Why, she wondered, couldn't she serve Mass with him?

It happened that Al caught a serious cold and had to stay home from school. It was his week to serve the 7 a.m. Mass before school. When altar boys were sick, they had to get substitutes. Al gave Ann Marie the list of substitute altar boys and asked her to go down the list until she found someone who could take his place. Ann Marie went down the list, and none of the boys could substitute. Some had colds. Others weren't home. A few just said, "It's too early for me." Ann Marie didn't tell her brother that she couldn't find a substitute. She had her own ideas.

The next morning Ann Marie went to the church. Waiting until Father Sam was already at the altar with no server, she hurriedly put on the traditional black and white uniform and marched out to assist the priest. Father Sam was concentrating on his prayers and at first didn't notice that his "altar boy" was really Ann Marie. It was only halfway through the Mass that he realized that a rule had been broken, that he had an "altar girl" for the first time in the history of his parish church.

After the Mass Father Sam asked Ann Marie why she broke the ancient rule of "boys only."

"My brother was sick," she explained. "I couldn't get a replacement. And since I'm the same flesh and blood as my brother, I didn't think you would mind."

With that answer Father Sam was speechless. He knew that the meaning of the Mass was Christ sharing his flesh and blood with the people, that there could be no second class citizens in the church. He realized that Ann Marie had acted with intelligence. But still, rules were rules. He had to give her a gentle admonition.

"It's okay for this once, Ann Marie. But please, not again! I must insist that only boys serve at this altar."

Ann Marie agreed.

Al got better and was able to complete his week of serving Mass. Ann Marie kept her promise to stay away from the altar.

It happened one day at the children's Mass that Father Sam stood with his back to the altar while he was telling a story. One of the candles started melting fast. The flame was going crazy. Father Sam couldn't see the problem and the two altar boys were fast asleep. The wild candle flame caught Father Sam's robe on fire. Ann Marie saw the problem, rushed to the altar, and threw her coat over Father Sam. The priest was not burned. He was only red from embarrassment. The girl he had told to stay away from the altar had saved him while his altar boys slept.

Father Sam kept Ann Marie at his side for the rest of the Mass. He told everyone how he had told her not to serve at the altar after she had taken her brother's place.

From that day on, Father Sam let Ann Marie stand by his side at Mass. He explained his new rule in the parish bulletin:

"My dear parishioners: In a sense I am departing from the ancient tradition of 'boys only' as altar servers. I feel that God speaks to us in strange ways. The other day while my altar boys slept, a girl saved me from being burned. She rushed to the altar even though I had told her to stay away from the altar. I had said, 'You can't serve.' But who can deny she did a great service to me? I have come to the conclusion that I need heads-up people around me at the altar. Girls may now serve at my Mass."

Except for a few people who didn't like any changes in the church, everyone accepted Father Sam's new tradition. And the boys in Al's class didn't dare to laugh when he called his sister his best friend.

The Alien's Victory

At the bottom of a beautiful snow-capped mountain, there is a town called Wildflower. It is a happy town today. But it was not a happy town at the time the Alien went there.

When the Alien went to Wildflower, there were two neighborhoods divided by a chainlink fence. One neighborhood was named "Poison"; the other was named "Fear." The people of Poison followed the teaching of Reverend I.C. Beam. The people of Fear rejected the reverend's teaching.

No one knew where the Alien came from. He just appeared one day. There was no doubt about the fact that he was truly from another world because ordinary humans don't have purple beards and green moustaches.

When the Alien first came to Wildflower, he talked to the people of both neighborhoods. He was concerned especially about the children. He asked the people of Poison about their children. He wondered why they never smiled. He wondered why the wildflowers didn't grow. He had many questions for the people of Poison. But they didn't want to talk. They could only say, "The Reverend I.C. Beam doesn't allow us to talk to strangers. So get lost, Mr. Alien."

When the Alien asked the people of Fear why things were so bad in Poison, they explained a little of their history to him.

"In the old days, we had no chainlink fence dividing our town. There were no neighborhoods named Poison and Fear. Everyone was nice to each other. And the wildflowers always grew everywhere. Then the Reverend came to town. He convinced half of our people that he had a message from God. He said that God told him to put balloons in the air above our town. Most of the people thought it was strange to put balloons in the air. But he started a business of making the balloons and put them in the air. That's how we got our chainlink fence and our town became divided into Poison and Fear."

"What's the purpose of the balloons?" asked the Alien. ("What's the purpose?" was the Alien's favorite question.)

"The Reverend I.C. says that they are 'prayer' balloons. He says that this is how God wants us to pray — by sending messages to heaven in the balloons."

"This is strange," said the Alien, "for the balloons block out much of the sunlight and the wildflowers no longer grow."

"That's right," explained the people of Fear. "But you haven't heard the worst yet, Mr. Alien. These are not just harmless balloons with prayers inside. They are full of the breath of Reverend I.C.'s mouth. He breathes poison. The people of our neighborhood are afraid to pull them down for fear they will pop and let out his breath on our land."

"I think you would be better off taking a chance and pulling down the balloons," said the Alien. "As things are now, you will all die from lack of sunlight."

"We want to take the balloons down," said the people. "But there are many among us who are afraid to do so. They are afraid to talk back to Reverend I.C. They are starting to believe they really need the balloons for good luck. They think that maybe God really did speak to Reverend I.C. They're just not sure. Anyway, the Reverend had promised to open a new balloon factory here so everyone can make a lot of money. You see, he has been traveling and convincing other villages to put up his prayer balloons."

The Alien was shocked when he heard this last statement.

"More balloons? Other villages?" A furrow of worry appeared on the Alien's face. He was deeply troubled. But he did not stay troubled for long. He began pulling down the balloons from the neighborhood of Poison. Soon everyone lost their fear and the people from both neighborhoods began pulling down balloons.

When the final balloon was down, the Reverend I.C. came back to town. He yelled and screamed, "You are anathema — anathema — anathema." (The people didn't know what "anathema" meant, but the Reverend always used the word when he was super angry.) He stomped his feet and told the people they would all die for taking down the balloons, but nothing happened. The sunlight came back to both neighborhoods and the wildflowers began to grow again.

The people of both neighborhoods were so happy with the Alien that they wanted to make him their mayor. But he said, "I cannot be your mayor. I am happy just to see you happy. And now I must leave you. For as long as there are people like Reverend I.C. spreading their poisonous breath to other villages, my work is not done."

Having said this the Alien disappeared. Perhaps you too will get a chance to see the Alien should the Reverend I.C. ever decide to put up balloons in your town.

LaBerge Muren

v-h-i-r-r-r'

The
Christmas
Cat

A girl lived alone with her father in a large and expensive suburban house. The girl had her own room with almost a hundred toys. She had dolls that could walk and talk and wet. She had stuffed animals that could roar and cry and do all the things allowed by batteries or windups. But the girl never played with her toys. What she wanted was a real, live cat like her mother once had.

"I will not have any animals in my house," said the girl's father. "I tolerated a cat while your mother was alive. But I just don't like cats. Ask me for anything, my dear daughter, but not a live cat."

It happened one day that the girl's friend brought some baby kittens to school. She asked the girl if she wanted one.

"My cat had seven babies. I must find homes for them."

"Oh, yes, I want one more than anything. Please give me one — any one. My father says I can't have one, but maybe he will change his mind and let me have one for awhile."

The girl picked out a grey kitten and took it home that afternoon after school. She made a little house for her kitten with a cardboard box and kept it in her room, waiting for her dad to arrive home.

When the girl's father saw the kitten, he was angry.

"The cat has got to go," he said.

"I know, Dad, but please let me keep him for just a few months until he is grown up and can live on his own. I can't just let a little kitten out into the street."

"What do you mean by 'a few months?'" asked the dad.

"Just three months until Christmas," said the girl. "I promise that on Christmas Eve I will give up my cat."

The father felt uncomfortable about the date of Christmas Eve. He couldn't figure out why his daughter would want to part with her cat on such a day of joy.

"Joseph and Mary didn't have a home on Christmas Eve, so that's why I picked that day to give away my cat," explained the girl.

The father thought for a moment and then said:

"Okay. It's a deal. You can keep the kitten until Christmas Eve, but not a day more. And I don't want you to tell me on Christmas Eve that it isn't fair to give away your cat. Understood?"

"Yes, Dad. I understand. It's a deal."

Now the girl was very intelligent. She had a plan for her kitten and she immediately began to put her plan into action. In the first phase of her plan, she fed her kitten only the best canned cat food. Each time she opened a can with her father's electric can-opener, the kitten came running to her. Within a few weeks, the kitten identified the sound of the can-opener with delicious food — "Whirr." No sooner did the sound of the electric can-opener fill the air than the kitten came running to the girl.

In the second phase of the kitten's training, the girl put the electric can-opener in her bedroom and the kitten outside. She opened the window above her bed and then turned on the can-opener. The kitten would immediately come through the window and on to her bed.

"You're such a smart kitten," said the little girl. "I just have one more thing to teach you in order to keep you forever. There will be times when I may not be able to buy you the canned food you love so much. You must learn to catch your own food."

It was the first of December and the girl wrote in her private diary: "My cat is ready for Christmas. Today he caught a mouse in the ivy in our back yard. I told him he could let it go, that I would give him something to eat. I know he understood me. Now all I have to do is buy Dad a new electric can-opener for Christmas so I can have the old one for my room. I don't think I will be telling my Dad a lie when I say I'm giving my cat to the streets. If my precious grey ball-of-fur wants to come through my window when I turn on the old electric can-opener, it will be my cat's decision."

On Christmas Eve the girl was quite pleased with herself when she gave her dad his present. He thought it was an unusual present and said, "I didn't think our old can-opener was broken."

"It isn't broken," said the girl. "I just want to have it — so I can experiment with it for a science project."

The girl didn't think this was a lie, since she considered what she was doing with her cat to be a real science project.

"By the way, where is your cat?" asked the father. "You remember our deal, don't you?"

"I know, Dad. I said goodbye to my cat today. I put him out my window and told him he was on his own, just like I will be on my own some day."

The father was a little surprised with this unusual answer by his daughter. But he didn't ask her any more questions. He assumed his daughter gave the cat to a friend. Little did he realize that the cat had been trained to wait outside the girl's room for the signal from the electric can-opener.

The girl and her father opened a few presents. One was a battery-operated mechanical cat.

"I thought you might want this," said the father. And since the toy didn't come with its own battery, he borrowed the one from the smoke alarm to demonstrate how it could "meow." The girl pretended she was pleased.

After watching a few Christmas specials on TV, the girl and her father retired to their separate bedrooms. The girl waited a few minutes until she heard her father snore. Then she turned on the electric can-opener just for a few seconds. As trained, her cat jumped in through her window, and within minutes both were fast asleep.

At midnight, when most children expect Santa to be visiting their homes, the cat began to scratch the girl's face. She at first thought she was dreaming, but then realized why she was scratched. There was smoke in her room. They had forgotten to unplug the Christmas tree lights and a fire had started. The smoke alarm with its missing battery did not function. With her cat tucked under her arm, the girl rushed to her father's room and woke him up. He quickly put out the fire. They were just in time to save their house.

As the three of them sat around their burnt Christmas tree, the father said, "I guess I was pretty silly asking you to get rid of your cat. How can I ever be mean to a hero who saved our lives?"

The girl's father held the cat in his lap and stroked it while the grey ball-of-fur purred its approval.

LaBerge Muren

How a Lizard
Conquered
a Dinosaur

In Singapore, there was a family of five lizards who lived behind a picture of the Arizona desert in Room 33 of the Bingo Hotel. They had an easy life, racing across the hotel walls chasing bugs to eat. The guests in Room 33 didn't know the lizards lived behind the picture on their wall. And the lizards were careful only to come out when there was no-one in the room.

The five lizards had nicknames. Papa was called "Socrates." Whenever he was asked a question, he would answer with another question. For example, when his children asked him, "Why must we always eat bugs?" he answered, "Why must fish always swim in water?" Mom was called "CC" because her favorite food was cookie crumbs. The three children were named after the neon sign whose light flashed on and off into Room 33. "Pep" was the oldest. He was lazy and slept most of the day. "See" was the middle kid. She had the strongest voice. "Cola" was the baby and the family clown. He would race across the ceiling when the guests were in the room. It was a daredevil stunt that got him into a lot of trouble with his family.

"Cola, you are endangering all of our lives," warned his father. But the youngster didn't know the meaning of "endanger." He just knew the meaning of fun.

Once Cola almost got his family into serious trouble. The year was 1953. That was the year when the Bingo hotel first put TVs in the rooms. The lizard family was no different from most human families in that they had never seen a TV before. One night the light from the magical picture box suddenly awakened them. They stuck their heads out from their home, the picture of the Arizona desert. The room guests were watching a movie called "The Battle of the Dinosaurs."

The lizard family watched the movie from the peep holes in their picture. They saw creatures like themselves fighting each other in the magic box. Even Papa Socrates couldn't explain why lizards called "dinosaurs" were fighting each other and making strange noises. The family stared silently — almost hypnotized — except for Cola, the family clown. He raced out from behind the picture across the ceiling and dropped right on the TV. Then he began to charge the TV screen as though he too was fighting the dinosaurs. As he charged the TV screen, he knocked himself senseless and the guests ran from the room, yelling: "Manager, manager, there's an awful lizard in our room."

By the time the guests returned with the manager to Room 33, Cola had revived himself and had joined his family in hiding behind the picture.

"That was a dumb thing to do, Cola," said his family. "You could have gotten us all killed. See the manager with the broom in his hand. That's his weapon to get rid of us."

"I'm sorry," cried Cola. "I just saw lizards fighting in the magic box. I thought I could break up the fight. But there were no lizards in the box. I hit glass. It was just a picture of lizards."

Though Socrates had never seen a TV movie before, he tried to explain what was happening from different conversations he had heard over the years. This is how he explained things to Cola and his family:

"I don't know anything about the magic box. But I do know that about 65 million years ago our forefathers controlled this earth. They were more than a thousand times our size. They were bigger than this hotel. Then one day something came out of the sky and hit the earth. There was a big explosion. A cloud of dust covered the earth and there was no more sunlight. There was no more grass and trees and our forefathers died."

"If our forefathers were so big, why are we so small?" asked Cola.

Socrates answered in his usual manner: "Why is not a leaf a tree?" Then he continued his explanation. "You see, our forefathers finished their job. The world no longer needed big guys. It only needed lizards, not dinosaurs."

"What was the job of the big guys?" asked Cola.

Socrates answered with a question: "How do Americans and Australians get to our hotel?"

"By taxi," answered CC.

"Right," said Socrates. "And taxis don't run on air. They need gasoline. And what is gasoline? It is a dinosaur in liquid form. The people who talk about these things call our forefathers 'fossil fuel.'"

The family of lizards was proud of their father's knowledge. And they were proud that their forefathers had played such a great part in making the modern world a happy place for the hotel guests of Room 33. But CC still had a question that was bothering her.

"My dear husband, can you please tell me what our purpose in life is now that we are no longer fuel for cars? Is our purpose simply to hide behind the picture in Room 33?"

CC's question was a good one. Socrates had to think for a minute. Finally, he answered with a question: "My dear wife, why did the great kings of the world have clowns in their courts?"

"But there is no king in Room 33," answered CC.

Socrates looked at all his children. He wanted them to understand their purpose in life. Finally Cola spoke up. "I know I'm here in Room 33 so people will forget how important they are. Maybe they will learn to laugh the next time I fight the monsters on their magic box."

Everyone was amazed that the baby of the family gave such a smart answer. But Socrates had the last word.

"While it is a good idea to make people laugh, son, I think for right now we better just be content in getting better at our game of hide and seek. Otherwise we might meet our doom at the end of a broom."

The family agreed with their dad. They had alot of fun in Room 33, but only when the guests were out or asleep.

LaBerge Muren

The
Santa Claus
Dream

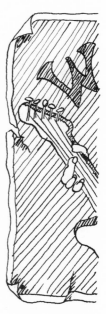

T here once lived a boy who had the same dream every night. In his dream Santa Claus called him with these words: "Come here, my friend, I need you to help me give away these presents to poor children."

The boy told his parents about the dream and they said; "That's a nice dream. But remember it is *only* a dream. We're sure Santa has enough elves to give away his presents to the poor children." (The boy's parents really didn't believe in Santa Claus, but only pretended to believe. A lot of adults are like that.)

The boy didn't argue with his parents. But in his heart he knew that Santa didn't have enough elves to help him. So he knew that if he ever had the chance, he would help Santa deliver gifts.

It happened one Christmas that the boy got many wonderful presents — an electric train, a bicycle, a football, roller skates, and many games. He played with his presents for a day and then gave them away to the poor children who attended his public school. A teacher from the school called his parents and told them what he had done.

"Your boy found who the poor children were and he gave away a football, a bicycle, an electric train, roller skates, and many other games. Do you approve of this?"

The boys parents were shocked at what their son had done. They discussed the situation with each other before talking to their son.

"What do you think got into the boy?" said his father. "Do you suppose he was obeying those crazy, so-called Santa Claus dreams he says he has been having? Do you think he needs professional help — like seeing a psychiatrist?"

"I don't know what to think," answered the mother. "He certainly doesn't have our values. I think he is influenced by the type of children in his school. I don't think he would have this problem of giving away his things if we found a nice private school for him. Let's find an expensive private school where there will be no poor children. In such a school, he will not be able to obey his Santa dream."

The father agreed with the mother's reasoning. That night they spoke to their boy.

"Son, we understand you gave away all your presents to the other children," said his father. "Your mother and I don't understand why you think the way you do. We have decided to send you to a private, Catholic school. The children there are from the same breeding as we. It will be good for you."

The boy didn't understand his father's speech. He knew nothing about "breeding" except what he learned in the second grade when his class went to a dairy farm and saw different breeds of cows. The boy cried a little because he didn't want to leave his friends at the public school. But he did as his parents wished. He had no other choice.

The boy found his new school a little strange at first. He wasn't used to having a Bible study class every day. He didn't know anything about religion. His only contact with the other world of spirits were his dreams of Santa Claus. He always had the Santa dream, even when it wasn't the Christmas season. And the dream was always the same — Santa calling him to help deliver presents to poor children.

It happened one day in Bible class that the teacher read the story of the rich young man who wanted to love God more perfectly. The boy was surprised to hear the advice given the rich young man: "Give away all your things to the poor people." The boy was so surprised by this kind of teaching that he said to his parents; "I learned in class that God likes my Santa dream."

The boy's parents were shocked by what he was learning in school. They knew they had to find another kind of private school for him. They searched and searched until they found a new school. It was named "The School of the Wiseman's Gold." After long talks with the school's principal, the boy's parents were assured that there would be no Bible lessons about rich young men being asked to give things to the poor.

The boy's father announced the change of schools with these words: "My son, I know you don't know anything about the evils of communism. You probably don't even know what the word means. But your mother and I don't want you to go to that communist-Catholic school. We want you to grow up to be a good American like ourselves. After all, we aren't Catholics, so there is no need for you to receive that kind of teaching."

The boy was sad, but again he did as his parents wished. In his new school, he was taught that God only blesses those who can hold a job and make a lot of money. The boy told this to his parents and they were happy with what he was learning. But each Christmas while their son was attending the "School of the Wiseman's Gold," their boy would still give away his presents.

The parents talked to the school counselor, even gave him money to help their son abandon his "crazy ideas" about giving away everything. The counselor just threw up his hands and said:

"I try to tell him that God blesses bankers and not bums. I try to tell him that God wants us to have the wealth of this earth. I taught him about the wealth of King Solomon. I made him watch the TV preachers and showed him pictures of their cars and expensive homes. I did my best to tell him that God favors the rich. But nothing works. He is stubborn. Maybe when he reaches the age of 18 he will be normal like us. Maybe he will want an expensive car for an expensive girlfriend. Then he won't think of giving away anything."

The boy did finally reach the age of 18 and graduated from the private school. He won a scholarship to a university and within six years he had earned a medical degree. The parents were happy with their son, the medical doctor, because he would be rich.

After he was a full-fledged doctor, the boy said to his parents, "Mom and Dad, I love you very much. But I am going to be a doctor in a faraway country where the people are very sick and have no money to pay me."

The boy's parents looked at each other and said, "Our son still has the Santa Claus dream."

It was true. He still had the same dream that he had as a child. And it is said that the poor people who sleep in his tent at the jungle medical station can actually hear sleigh bells ring when he sleeps and dreams.

LaBerge Muren

The
Two
Brothers

T here was once a father who raised two sons. The older son was athletic, tall, handsome, and popular with girls. The younger son was not too athletic, handsome, or popular. The older son didn't study much but always got A's in school. (His girlfriends usually did his homework for him.) He was a smooth-talker who managed to convince his teachers he deserved A's. He was also the star of the basketball team and had many worshipping fans. He took advantage of his popularity and borrowed money (which he never paid back) from his worshipping fans. Indeed, the older son was talented, but he used his talents to get what he wanted from others.

The younger son had to struggle to get C's in school. He was kept on the basketball team only out of pity by the coach. He never got to play and usually had to hand out towels to the players after the game. When people talked about him, he was always called "the *brother* of the basketball star."

The father tried not to spoil his sons. At home they were supposed to share chores — doing dishes, taking out the garbage, and cleaning their rooms. Since the older brother always had plenty of money from his many admirers, he forced his younger brother to do his work. The father wasn't supposed to know of this arrangement. "If you tell dad, I'll hit you," warned the older brother.

The father loved both of his sons, but it seemed to the younger son as if he loved his brother better. He went to all the basketball games and cheered louder than anyone when his son scored. At home he never had an argument with his basketball star son. And the older son was always polite. It was always "Yes, Dad, I'd be happy to take out the garbage." But when his dad wasn't looking, he'd twist his younger brother's arm until he took out the garbage.

The younger brother never told his dad about the "arrangement" of doing his brother's jobs. But when he was frustrated, he would go to his room and have a temper tantrum. Once he was so angry when he had to do the dishes, take out the garbage, and clean the bathrooms, that he punched a hole in his bedroom wall with his bare fist. Although he was punished by his dad for the hole in the wall, he never told him why he did it. He accepted the fact that he would always be second place to his brother and second best-loved by his dad.

When the oldest son was seventeen and the younger one was fifteen, the father was unexpectedly killed in an auto accident. Both boys were sad. Yet at the funeral the older son felt embarrassed when his brother cried out loud. The older brother was sad, but his thoughts were now on all the things he would do with the money from the dad's will.

A few days after the funeral, the boys' aunt brought them to the attorney to discuss the father's will. The older brother was very interested in his father's will and asked the attorney to read it out loud. This was the will:

"To my older son I leave my Bible. I treasured this book very highly. I hope he reads it and understands it. To my younger son I leave all my material possessions - home, car, and savings. These things will come to him on his twenty-first birthday. I am confident he will share what he has with the less fortunate. I always realized his life was difficult, having to live in the shadow of his older brother. I was aware of the "arrangement" made for doing dishes, etc. I'm sure my older son will always be able to take care of himself and does not need my charity."

For the first time the younger brother realized how much his dad loved him. He put his arm around his saddened older brother and said:

"Relax. We have six years to think about how this money is to be used. Maybe during those six years we can learn to be brothers. Don't you think that's what Dad really wanted?"

"You're right," said the older brother. "I guess it's my turn to wash the dishes tonight."

LaBerge Muren

Shared
Water

In the old days, beavers and skunks of Hidden Valley did not associate with each other. They weren't enemies. But they weren't friends, either. They simply lived on opposite sides of the river and never saw each other except from a distance. Then something happened that threw them together. Something happened that changed their world forever.

To understand what happened, you must know that the sky had given no rain for three years. The fields had lost their beautiful wildflowers. Birds abandoned their nests and flew North in search of water. Foxes, rats, and most other creatures went south. The only animals who stayed behind were skunks and beavers. They, too, were fearful of dying of thirst.

At this time of danger, a beaver named Giovanni challenged his fellow beavers with a plan for survival. In the special way beavers communicate by moving their jaws, he said, "My brothers and sisters, we must change our way of life. Up to now we have been building tiny, teeny dams. But these little dams don't help us in dry times like now. If we want to live, if we want our children to live, we must build a giant dam where water can be stored for many years."

The beavers of the Valley shook their heads up and down and wagged their tails to agree. They liked Giovanni's plan and agreed to help him build the giant dam. That afternoon they all began to collect sticks. During the next few days, they collected thousands of sticks and began plastering them into a wall with whatever mud was left in the dried-out river. Even the baby beavers who loved to just play with the mud helped out. The beavers worked hard for a week and were almost done with the dam when great storm clouds appeared in the sky. Giovanni was happy to see the rain clouds, but he was also worried. If the rains came before the dam was finished, the dam would break and all their work would be ruined. He urged his brother and sister beavers to work hard while he went out to look for more workers. He knew that he could finish the dam that afternoon before the rains came if only he had about a hundred more workers.

Giovanni knew that the only other animals left in Hidden Valley were the skunks. Though he had never gotten close to a skunk before, he knew he had to now. So that's what he did. He went to the skunks and asked for help. He explained to the skunks that they would have the same privileges of drinking from the water of the giant dam. They could drink the dam water and use the dam mud for years and years to come. The skunks agreed to help. They followed Giovanni to the dam and worked for three solid hours until it began raining. It was because of their help that the dam was finished as soon as it began raining. The skies poured for three days and nights and the giant dam quickly filled. Giovanni was happy. The skunks were happy. But not all of the beavers were happy. The unhappy beavers were led by a cousin of Giovanni. His name was Girardia.

Girardia was so angry he wanted to tear down the dam.

"Why did you make a deal with the skunks?" he asked Giovanni. "They came in at the last minute to do a little work and you gave them rights to the water. We don't want our children playing with their children. We don't want to share the same drinking and bathing areas. Beavers are beavers and skunks are skunks. This is our dam, not theirs. You must tell the skunks they have to go, or else!"

Giovanni was not afraid of Girardia. He knew Girardia very well. He knew that Girardia had been the pet of a rich family from the Big City and was fed steak every night. He knew that Girardia had picked up many human habits before his owners had to give him up.

"Look Girardia," answered Giovanni. "I know the Valley is not like New York City. And I know you were accustomed to doing things a different way when you were a pet. But out here it is different. I'm not changing my mind. We can live in peace with the skunks. I made them a promise and I will keep my promise. I don't care if they only worked a few hours on the dam. I needed their help and they get the reward I promised."

"I will not live with you or the skunks," said Girardia. "I will take my family outside of the dam. I don't ever want to see you again.'

So that's what Girardia did. He took his family outside, downstream from the dam. There he built a fence so that he couldn't see the skunks or the other beavers. And to this very day Girardia and his descendents live inside a fenced area outside the dam where the water flows down to the Valley.

If you should ever go to Hidden Valley, you will see the giant dam high above in the distance. And down from the dam you will see the fenced in area of Girardia and his followers. But I must warn you. If you are thirsty, drink water from the dam. For the water that passes by the homes of Girardia and his followers is bad, and will make you sick.

LaBerge Muren

Sidestepper

Long ago some people decided to follow a light that appeared to be moving in the sky. These were the days before airplanes or UFO's. These people studied the skies and knew that the moving light would lead them to a most special newborn baby. For this reason the people were called "wisemen": they understood the importance of a newborn baby.

Before the wisemen left their home village, they packed presents to give the newborn child. Among the gifts were stuffed animals, some sweet smelling spices, and a little golddust. So many were the stuffed animals they gathered that they brought along an extra camel just to carry them.

As they began their trip, the wisemen noticed that their baggage camel was pregnant.

They said, "It is not fair to make this mother camel carry all these stuffed animals. Let's give away all the stuffed animals to children along the way. By the time we reach the special child of our star, we will have a real live baby camel to give him." They agreed it was a great idea.

The wisemen were on the road for several weeks. They met many poor children and gave them the stuffed animals — giraffes, elephants, foxes, walruses, mice and chickens. Each day they seemed to be getting closer and closer to their destination, though they themselves had to admit, it was not easy trying to follow a moving light in the sky.

After a few weeks the light in the sky seemed to come to a rest.

"Our special light is resting," said the wisemen to each other, "and so must we." So that's what they did. And it was at this time that their baggage camel gave birth to its baby.

Almost instantly after its birth, the baby camel began to walk. The wisemen cheered the little creature as he struggled to get on his feet and follow his mother. But after a few days the wisemen noticed something strange. It seemed that one of the baby camel's hind legs was shorter than the other.

"The little guy can't walk in a straight line," they observed. It was a fact. The baby camel could not walk in a straight line. For this reason the wisemen named him "Sidestepper." Though the baby tried to walk in a straight line, he was in fact always walking in half circles.

The wisemen were smart people, but they did one dumb thing on their trip. When the light appeared to stop in the sky, they went to the local police station to ask if anyone knew where the special child should be. The police took the wisemen to the king who was a very jealous and cruel man.

"So you are looking for a special child," said the king. "No one is really special in my kingdom unless he is born in my palace. I too am interested in your so-called special child. When you find him, come back and tell me where he is so I too may go and pay my respects."

The wisemen could tell by the tone of the king's voice that he was an insincere and evil man. So they went their way in search of the child but resolved never to report to the king.

With the help of some children who had seen the special child, the wisemen finally found him with his mother and father living in a cave on a hillside. With great respect, they entered the cave and presented their gifts to the parents of the child — a little gold-dust, some spices, and the baby camel, Sidestepper.

The wisemen warned the parents about the question the king had asked them. And after a few days of visiting, they went back to their own land.

A few days later, the father and mother said good-bye to all the people who had been visiting them. They knew that they had to go to another country to escape the evil king, who was jealous of their child. The children brought them new rumors that this king was so evil, he would kill children.

As they walked along the dusty trail to another land, the father said to his wife: "I hope our camel doesn't slow us down. He seems to be going in a lot of different directions. I've never seen a camel who couldn't walk straight. I only wish we weren't in such a hurry to escape this evil king."

"Don't worry," said his wife. "I believe Sidestepper is a special animal. He is our special 'star' to guide us to a land of safety."

Meanwhile the jealous and cruel king realized that the wisemen were not coming back to give him a report. Like a crazy person, he ordered his police to kill all the newborn baby boys in his neighborhood. "Kill the baby of these wisemen, the one who dares to take my power. I alone am king! I alone will remain king!" shouted the evil king.

While the king's special police were doing their evil work, one of them saw the footprints of Sidestepper and the family.

"Look at these unusual footprints," said the policeman to one of his friends. "These are the prints of an animal that can't walk straight. It must be a crippled animal. Should we report this finding to the king?"

The policeman's friend just laughed. "Why would the king be interested in a family with a crippled animal? Have you ever heard of a family of a king that had to keep a lame animal? It would be silly to follow these footprints."

The policeman agreed. They never told the king.

After several days of difficult travel, the little family arrived in another country where they were safe from the evil king. And they stayed in that land for a while, thanking God for all the gifts they had been given — especially their precious camel who couldn't walk a straight line.

La Berge Muren

The Heaven Climber

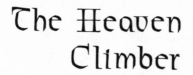

Z was a small boy, but he was very smart. His classmates called him "Z Big Brain." Besides being very smart, Z was very generous in helping others. Those who did poorly in his class could always go to him for help. Without the help of a calculator, Z could add large columns of numbers in his head. He was so good at math, his teachers predicted that he would be some kind of banker, tax-collector, or scientist. Not only was he good in math, but he also did well in his other subjects — especially nature study. He knew the names of hundreds of types of trees and plants. Even when his teacher forgot names, Z always had the answer: "This is an apple tree; that is a sycamore tree."

Z hardly ever had problems at school. But once in the fourth grade he got in trouble with his mother for wearing home an expensive sweater that didn't belong to him.

"I don't know where you got that sweater," said his mother. "But I want you to return it immediately to its owner."

"But mom," complained Z. "I won the sweater from my friend on a fair bet. I bet the boy next to me that I would get 100 percent on my math test. I won the bet, which was for his sweater. If I had lost, I would have given him my hat. It was a fair bet. I didn't steal the sweater."

"I don't want you to gamble. Return the sweater, apologize, and give the boy this cake."

Z obeyed his mother. The boy was glad to get back his sweater and the cake.

In the seventh grade, Z had trouble with the school bully, an oversized boy called "Boa." Everyday at recess and noon-hour, Boa would chase Z and hit him. It always happened when the yard supervisor wasn't looking. But Z learned how to get away from Boa by climbing trees. Boa was not strong enough to climb trees. He was only good at sitting on those smaller than himself and punching them. It was because of Boa that Z became the best treeclimber in his school.

Z liked to climb trees even when Boa wasn't chasing him. Once his mother called him at dinner time, "Son, come down from that tree. Your food is getting cold."

And Z answered, "I'm happy up here. Do you think I was meant to be a monkey? Why do I love to climb trees?"

"I don't know whether you're part monkey," answered his mother. "You probably love trees because you feel closer to heaven. But I still want you to come down and eat your dinner."

As Z was climbing down, he asked his mother: "Do you think I can ever climb high enough to see the face of God?"

His mother was surprised by the question. She thought about the danger of Z climbing any higher. "You don't have to climb a very big tree to see God."

Z grew from boyhood to manhood but always remained very short. But what he lacked in size, he made up for in hard work. As a teacher once prophesied, he became a successful tax-collector.

It happened one day while Z was out collecting taxes that a large crowd gathered on his street. The people were surrounding a young man. Most of the people were trying to touch the man.

Z asked someone, "What's going on?"

"This is the teacher from Nazareth. Power comes from him. He heals with the touch of his hands those who believe in his message."

"What is his message?" asked Z.

"It's simple: All the people of earth are children of the same Father in heaven."

When Z heard this, he too wanted to see and touch the teacher from Nazareth. Never had he heard any of the religious leaders dare teach that all the nations were children of one God. So he quickly climbed a tree to see the teacher as he passed by.

When the teacher passed underneath the tree, he looked up and stared into the eyes of Z.

"Come down, Z. I wish to join you for dinner tonight."

Z was so surprised by the invitation, he almost fell from the tree. Nobody ever wanted to eat with him. Most people hated him because he was a tax-collector. People usually cursed him. But the teacher asked him in a nice way to share a meal.

Z climbed down the tree and welcomed the teacher into his home. No sooner had he sat down to dinner when someone started pounding on his door so hard it almost broke. When he opened the door, he saw an angry man dressed in the clothes of a church teacher. Z recognized the man, someone he had not seen for twenty years. It was Boa, the school bully.

"You let this upstart teacher from Nazareth into your home? Why? Don't you know he teaches against my church? He calls me a 'big bag of dead men's bones.' He's ruining my business ... I mean, church. If you make friends with him, Mr. Z, I will make your life miserable. It will be just like the old times in grade school."

Z tried to invite Boa in for dinner. But Boa just tore his own shirt like a crazy person and called Z names.

At dinner that evening, the young teacher from Nazareth explained to Z how important it was for rich people to share their wealth with the poor. He convinced Z that the people who had nothing would be the welcome guests in God's house.

As he said good-bye to the teacher, Z promised he would share all his wealth with the poor.

In bed that evening, Z started thinking about his grade school, about Boa, about his mother, and all the times she called him from his tree for dinner. Then he remembered the words she had spoken: "You won't have to climb a very big tree to see God."

Z knew his mother's words had come true this day.

LaBerge Muren

Why
the Wolves
Howl

At the edge of the desert, there once lived
a family of wolves. Like most wolf
families, they were very tight knit —
not like the lone wolves of storybooks. They
spent their days gathering food and taking care
of their young. They had no desire to kill
humans or change themselves into monsters
while the moon was full. They were simply
the gentle, shy animals God had made them to
be.

For their fun, this family of wolves loved to visit the campfires of their distant relatives — the human family. They knew they were not welcome close to campfires, so they always stayed their distance. They also knew that because of false stories, people would be afraid of them and want to kill them. "The human family," warned the wise old wolves, "always kills what they fear."

One evening at the very place where the forest meets the desert by the river, the wolf family saw a large gathering of people by a bonfire. A man dressed in long robes was speaking to the people from a tree trunk. The family went as close as they could and hid behind some rocks. There were soldiers in the crowd and other people who looked very important — business people, religious leaders, and politicians.

"This Carpenter who goes around telling our people not to slaughter animals in our Temple, this Carpenter who says he can destroy our Temple and rebuild it in three days — he must die."

The wolves were frightened by the fierce expression on the face of the man standing on the tree trunk. They had heard about the Carpenter from the Owl. The Owl got his information from the pigeons, doves, and sheep. They knew the Carpenter was in trouble for ruining the business of those who captured the birds to sell them for church worship ceremonies. The wolves had been curious about this Carpenter who seemed so much in tune with their animal world. They would have gladly let him into their family, where he could have lived in peace. The wolf family had once seen this Carpenter at the river when he released a fox from a hunter's trap and set him free. They had heard the man's words to the fox: "Friend of my Father, go free; the human fox is not as nice as thee."

The wolves were plainly upset by the sermon of the man standing on the tree trunk. They looked at each other in a way that only wolves truly understand. The moon was full and they wanted to howl. They wanted their cry to fill the evening air and let the world know that there was something very wrong going on at the human campfire. But they waited.

These were the days before wolves actually howled. Patiently, they remained silent. The man on the tree stump, who seemed to be in love with his own voice, was still talking.

"This Carpenter has an evil spirit. He tells the people not to listen to me. He tells the people they no longer have to buy the pigeons and doves to be killed in my church. If those who sell the animals go broke, then we all lose money. This Carpenter preaches an evil doctrine. He must die."

The wolf family didn't understand much about the religion of the human family. They didn't know much about evil spirits. Their only experience was that of the Great Spirit who gave them life and preserved the order of nature. They did not know the meaning of "being broke" or "he must die" and many of the other things the preacher talked about. But they did sense that the man talking from the tree stump wanted to do something very bad. They were afraid for themselves and for the whole forest.

When the man on the tree stump finished talking, the wolves let out a cry that could be heard for miles away. Their cry was their way of saying, "We don't like what is going on." The wolves knew that one of their fellow animals — the human — was breaking the law of the Great Spirit of their forest.

So, today, when you hear the cry of wolves under a full moon, remember why they howl. They are telling us humans that there is something wrong with the way we treat each other.

The Strongman

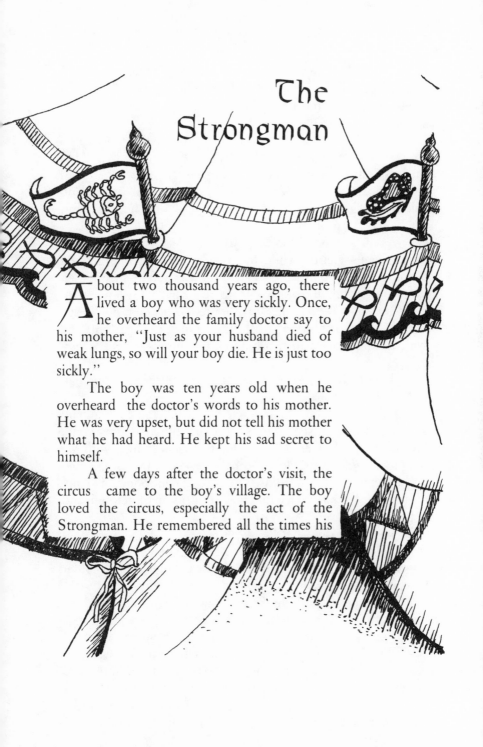

About two thousand years ago, there lived a boy who was very sickly. Once, he overheard the family doctor say to his mother, "Just as your husband died of weak lungs, so will your boy die. He is just too sickly."

The boy was ten years old when he overheard the doctor's words to his mother. He was very upset, but did not tell his mother what he had heard. He kept his sad secret to himself.

A few days after the doctor's visit, the circus came to the boy's village. The boy loved the circus, especially the act of the Strongman. He remembered all the times his father had taken him to the circus each year when it came to the village. He knew his mother would not take him. She would say, "You must stay home. You are too sickly to go to the circus."

So the boy did not ask his mother for permission to go to the circus. He waited until she was asleep one night and left on his own. He had no money, but he felt certain he could sneak in under the fence. A small and sickly boy could do things like get under fences, whereas big and healthy boys might have a problem.

As luck would have it, the boy was caught by the Strongman's guards while he was trying to get under the fence. The two guards cursed and hit the boy. The Strongman came out of his dressing room to see what was happening.

"Leave the kid alone," he shouted to his guards. "Leave the kid alone or you will wish you hadn't touched him," he warned in a voice which prompted the guards to let the boy go.

The sickly boy started to apologize, but the Strongman didn't let him speak.

"You can come to my act free," said the Strongman. The boy was surprised, not only by what the Strongman said, but by how he looked. He was not an oversized man with the bulging muscles of modern football players and wrestlers who build themselves on steroids. The Strongman looked like any other man. He had a face that was at the same time tough and gentle.

The boy could hardly speak.

"Thank you," he said. "I want to be like you. My doctor says I am to die soon because I have weak lungs like my father who died ... "

"Nonsense," said the Strongman. "We weren't made to die, but to live. I, too, was weak as a child, but my father hardened me. He always made me lift something more than I could lift. My father had me wrestle with him, and when he was away I wrestled with the trees. We ran in the snow and swam the cold rivers. My father would never let me think I was sickly. I was not born strong; I became strong with the firmness and determination of my father, who would not allow me to fail."

The boy was spellbound by the words of the Strongman. He had never heard a man speak like this before. For the first time since his own father's death, he felt good about himself. He hesitated for a moment and then said asked the Strongman, "Please sir, can I stay with you? I could chop wood for you and cook your meals. If you could teach me what you learned from your father, I too could be strong some day."

"Only if your mother says you can come with me," answered the Strongman, confident that the boy's mother would say "no."

"I'll go ask my mother," promised the boy. "I'll be right back."

The boy ran off into the night. But he didn't go home. He simply hid in the bushes for an hour and then returned. He knew his mother would never give him permission to live with the Strongman. So he had to tell this lie to save his life.

"My mother said it is okay," said the boy to the strongman.

And the Strongman, though surprised, kept his promise.

So the boy began his new life. His mother wept for him, thinking he had drowned in the river. The boy knew his mother would be sad. But he thought of the day when he cold return to his home and present himself as a strong boy, not the sickly child.

The Strongman gave the boy a daily routine to follow. He made him lift buckets of sand and each day he increased the amounts put in the buckets. He wouldn't let the boy eat what other children ate. "You can't put junk food in your body and not be junk yourself," was one of the Strongman's sayings. Each day the boy lifted more weight and ran more miles. Sometimes he was tempted to run away and go to his mother. But he stayed with the Strongman.

After a year the Strongman was pleased with the boy's health. "You can lift twice your own weight, my son. You can run ten miles and not be out of breath. You know how to breathe, eat, and sleep properly. It's time you went back to your Mother. It is not right to keep her sad any longer."

The boy returned to his home. His mother was still in mourning, convinced that he had drowned in the river. At first she did not believe it was him, but only a healthy boy who looked like her son. After embracing, he told her of his year with the gentle Strongman.

As he grew older, the boy traveled to foreign lands. Now he told his mother where he was going. He was fascinated by the people of other lands. He went to India and Japan. And wherever he went, he made it a point to visit the strongmen of the area and learn their secrets of strength.

Once, while he was visiting the country of Palestine, he entered the ancient city of Jerusalem. There were a lot of people on the streets this particular day. The young man sensed that there was something strange and unusual going on. The people had that same kind of strange look in their eyes as those who come to the circus. He started to ask a man what was going on, why the people had this strange look in their eyes. But just then a soldier of the Roman army grabbed his arm and shouted to another soldier: "Here's a kid who looks strong enough. And he's a foreigner, so we can use him."

The young man didn't understand the language of the soldier and protested, "Leave me alone. I have done nothing wrong."

While the young man was struggling with the soldier, one from the crowd who knew the young man's language explained what was going on: "A prisoner is on his way to be executed. The prisoner is too weak to carry the heavy wood placed on his shoulders. The soldier wants you to carry it because you are a foreigner. Just do it to save yourself trouble."

The young man now stood face to face with the prisoner. He hadn't seen this poor, condemned man before. But as he looked into his eyes, he saw his friend: the Strongman. Very few people had eyes like that, eyes which communicated the meaning of life.

The prisoner spoke: "Lift this weight and you will be strong. Lift this weight and you will never die."

The young man had remembered the teaching of the Strongman. He remembered how as a child he was so afraid of dying and how the Strongman had given him a new life.

The young man took the heavy weight of the wood on his shoulders and walked up the hill with the prisoner. And the promise of the prisoner came true: The young man didn't die!

LaBerge Muren

The Lucky Lamb

There once was a lamb who dreamed of adventure. She didn't like the idea of just being "one of the flock."

"Must I spend all of my days eating grass?" she complained to the sheep and rams. The others didn't answer her. They just gave her a look that said: "Lambs are lambs and dogs are dogs; don't try to be anything else."

The lamb didn't give up her dream of seeking adventure. One day while the flock was grazing, she noticed that the shepherd and his dog were sleeping. Before, when she had tried to wander off, the shepherd always went after her.

"Now," she thought to herself, "is my big chance to find adventure in the distant hills while my shepherd sleeps."

And so the lamb crept quietly through the tall grass away from the flock, away from everything she had known, while the shepherd and his dog slept.

As the lamb approached the hills, a big-horned goat in his mountain cave saw her approaching.

"This is unusual," he said to himself. "The shepherd and his dog must be asleep. This poor lamb must be lost and frightened."

The goat climbed down from his rocky den to greet the lamb.

"You are lost and frightened," said the goat to the lamb, "but don't worry, I will help you get back to your flock. The mountain rocks are no place for you."

"I'm not lost or frightened," said the lamb. "I want to be here in the mountains. I'm bored with the tall grass of the flat-lands. But I would appreciate your help."

The goat was puzzled. He had always thought of sheep as dull creatures, stupid followers — not adventuresome like this little creature. Yet he thought it his duty to persuade the lamb to go back.

"You won't be able to live here, little lamb. Nature hasn't given you the right kind of legs and hooves to climb these rocks. But if you insist on seeing my world, I'll carry you on my back. You can stay for a while."

The lamb was happy with the goat's offer and quickly boarded his back for her ride up the hill to the goat's cave, his "hideout" as he called it.

After a few days in the goat's cave, the lamb became bored.

"I don't care if I never see another rock," she grumbled to herself. "And this food the goat gives me — leaves from some bush — is very boring."

The lamb told the goat she wanted to go back to the flock, but the goat told her that it was too dangerous for him to carry her downhill.

"I might slip and we would both be killed," complained the mountain goat. There was some truth in what he said.

No sooner had the goat spoken these words, when the noon skies grew dark. There was a great rumbling sound. The two peeked out of the cave and saw rocks coming down the hillside like rain. The ground shook and the rocks kept falling. For the first time in his life, the goat was afraid.

"This is most unusual," said the goat to the lamb. "I fear you have brought me bad luck."

The ground stopped shaking and the sun again appeared in the sky. The goat and the lamb heard the footsteps of people nearby.

"Perhaps it is your shepherd coming after you," said the goat.

They looked out of the cave. They saw no shepherd. Instead they saw a few people carrying the lifeless body of a man into a cave across the way. They watched the woman put some spices on the body of the man and then wrap him in a clean cloth. After they were finished, two soldiers in uniform pushed a rock across the entrance of the cave and sealed it with a special kind of wax. Then the soldiers sat down by the rock.

"This is really weird," said the goat. "First there is the darkness and the shaking of the mountain with a rainstorm of rock. And now there are these strange soldiers guarding a dead man. What can it mean?"

"I don't know," stuttered the lamb. For the first time in her life, she was afraid. "I wa-wa-wanted an adventure, but this is too scary. Please take me back, Mr. Goat."

"I can't take you back," said the goat. "See those soldiers guarding the rock across the way. They would love to have barbecued lamb. We must stay silent and hide for now."

The goat and lamb couldn't sleep that night for fear of all the strange things that happened that afternoon. The night seemed to last forever. Finally, their eyelids could stay open no longer and they fell asleep. The lamb dreamed of her happy days grazing under the watchful eye of her shepherd. The goat dreamed of his happy days climbing up and down his rocky hillside. Then suddenly, as though they were still in dreamland, they were awakened by a bright light. This light was brighter than the noonday sun.

"I've never slept till noon in my life," said the goat as he shielded his eyes as best he could.

The goat and the lamb had to turn away from the bright light that entered their cave. Then they heard a voice.

"Is my lamb here? It's time to go back to the fields."

"It's your shepherd," said the goat excitedly. "Your shepherd came to take you back. The light dimmed somewhat and the two animals looked up to see the shepherd.

The shepherd picked up his lamb, carried her out of the cave, and began walking down the rocky hillside. The goat looked across the way at the cave that was sealed by a rock. The cave was now open and the soldiers were gone. The goat looked down the hill and saw the soldiers running as though they had seen a ghost. The goat had tears in his eyes as he watched the shepherd and lamb disappear after a few minutes.

"I sure don't know what's been going on around here the past few days," thought the goat. "But that lamb sure is lucky, and I'm happy that she's back home."

LaBerge Muren

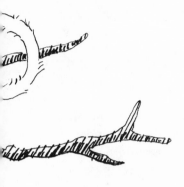

The World of Kings

O nce there was a Lion who was proud of his position as "King of All Beasts."

In his old age, this lion loved to hear stories about kings from the human world. And so he invited into his den any animal who had an experience with a king.

One evening, a Horse and Donkey who were good friends went to the Lion's den to tell their stories. The Horse told his story first.

"I once carried a king upon my back. This king called himself the Emperor, the Greatest King of All. This king would ride me into his stadium to begin his games ... "

At this point the Horse hesitated to go on with his story and said, "I don't know if you really want to hear my story, for this king was really not a very nice person."

"Go on," said the Lion. "I don't have a weak stomach. I'm able to hear any kind of a story. But just don't try to make up things; I only want to hear true stories."

"All right," said the Horse. "I'll continue. This emperor spent all the people's money on his games. He loved most of all the chariot races. The best athletes and horses of the world would compete on his racetrack. As the games became more popular, he wanted a bigger stadium in a bigger city. So what he did was burn down his old stadium along with the city, so his people would pay for a larger and more beautiful place for him to have his games."

"Why didn't the people get rid of this crazy emperor who burned down their city?" asked the puzzled Lion.

"Because he blamed the fire on some poor people who said our Great Spirit was their true king. These are the same people who try to protect us and our Forests," explained the Horse.

"Is that all you have to say about this emperor?" asked the Lion.

"Well, I wish it was," the Horse answered. "But if you want the truth, I must tell you that this person did very bad things to lions as well as the people. He starved the lions and then dressed these people he blamed for the fire in animal skins ... "

"Stop your story right there," said the Lion. "It is too brutal a story. I will never understand the human king such as the one you describe. Let me hear the Donkey's story."

"I, too, carried a king on my back," explained the Donkey. "But he was not an emperor like the Horse's. My king didn't have a city or a palace. He didn't even have a house. He slept outside most of the time like we do. He didn't have any money or armies or circuses. He would never have starved a lion and turned him on one of his fellow humans."

"So, in other words, your king was really not like the man the Horse spoke of," said the Lion.

"That's right," continued the Donkey. "I remember the day I gave him a ride. The other donkeys thought it was a joke. They told me that kings always rode on horses, not donkeys. But the truth is, my King rode on my back and all the people put palm branches along the road and sang for him as we went in triumph into the capitol city."

"What was the triumph?" asked the Lion. "Had he conquered other countries?"

"Like I said, my King had no army; so conquering other countries was just not his thing. I heard it explained that he only wanted to 'conquer hearts.' That's the human way of saying that he only wanted others to respect each other. His people loved him except for a few. And the few were like the emperor who burned down the city. The few killed him."

"Enough, enough of these stories," said the Lion and he let out a roar that shook the forest trees.

The Horse and the Donkey quietly departed, leaving the Lion to himself and his counselor, the Owl.

"I understand power," said the Lion to the Owl, "but I don't understand this thing called 'cruelty' in the animal called 'human.' Can you explain these matters to me in a way a Lion's head can understand?"

"I will do my best," said the Owl. "But of course you must remember this: If humans cannot understand each other, it may be impossible for us also.'"

"Let us at least try," begged the Lion, "for our survival in the forest seems to depend on these humans. Maybe there is something we should be doing differently."

"My Lion, I'm afraid there's not much we can do. The Great Spirit of the forest gave the human animal control over us. You see, my King, the human creature is not like any other species. For while a lion will always be a lion, and a fox will always be a fox, the human can change himself into something he was not born to be."

"You mean it would be like a mouse who could change himself into an elephant?"

"Yes, it is something like that. It is a kind of evil magic. For the sake of understanding, let us call the human animal an 'Alpha.' Every human is born to be an Alpha. He is meant to be like the King who rode on the Donkey's back. But the Alpha has something in his blood, something that no animal has. It is a kind of magic that can be good or evil. He can change himself into an Omega — like the emperor who rode on the Horse's back in his circus where he fed other humans to starved lions."

"I'm beginning to understand," said the Lion. "I must have more explanation."

And so the Owl continued explaining to the Lion all through the night until "the King of All Beasts'" eyelids grew heavy with sleep. For it always happens when the Owl starts talking about the Alpha and the Omega in the human animal, his listeners get so tired trying to understand his difficult words that they fall asleep.

The End